Library of Congress Cataloging-in-Publication Data available.
ISBN: 978-1-7331009-0-8

Meet the author and illustrator
www.jjobear.com

Table of Contents

Conclusion

Introduction

"The Art Of War" was written to guide kings and warriors on how to win battles in war. But because the lessons that the master Sun Tsu teaches are principles on how to be strategic, the advice is still relevant to help resolve all kinds of conflict, even those in everyday life.

Often times when we run into conflict, it's easy to be stuck in worry and doubt, but if you understand the simple concepts from "The Art Of War", it can help you in positioning yourself to win without engaging in dispute. That is the highest form of winning, it is the way of strategic thinking.

Let us follow the cat on her journey to learning how to strategize.

This is Misty

This is how she feels
during the course of
a day, there are highs

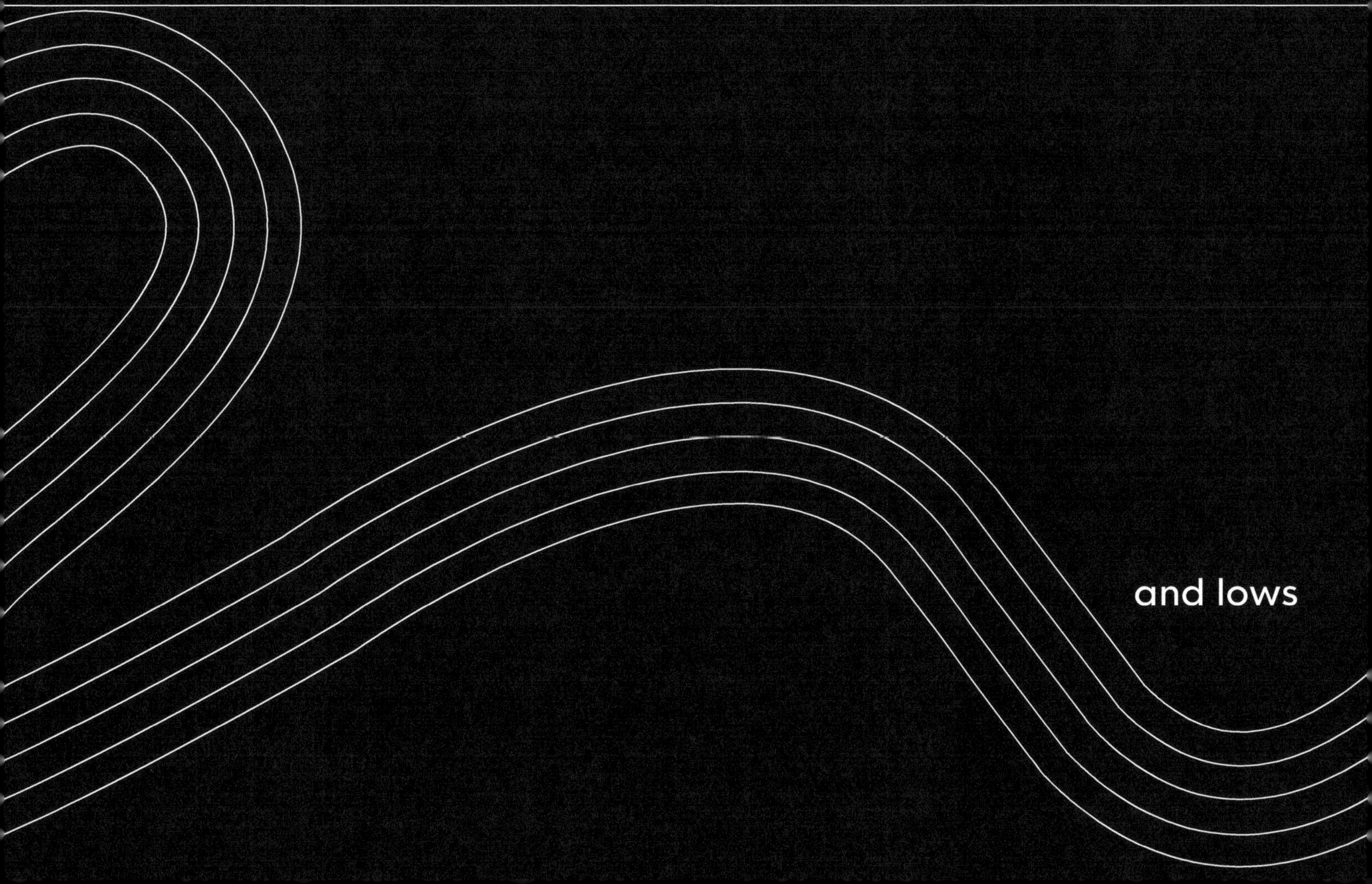

and lows

One day she found
a dog blocking
her path

And she
fell
down

down

down

in fear

She was caught
in this funky mood

Sun Zhu

Then she decided to seek out
Master Sun Zhu for help

Lessons

Learn these lessons and you need not
be in fear ever again...

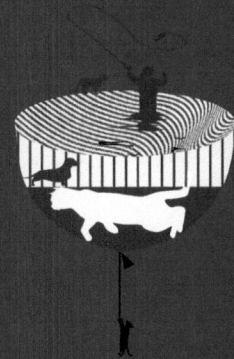

#1 Know Yourself and Your Enemy

If you know both yourself and the enemy, you can fight 100 battles without danger of defeat.

If ignorant of the enemy only knowing yourself, chances of winning and losing are equal.

If oblivious to both yourself and the enemy, you will be defeated every time.

#2 Win Without Destroying

Winning 100 victories and 100 battles does not count as real excellence.

The supreme
art of war is
winning without
fighting.

#3 Avoid the Strong, Attack the Weak

If equal, engage them

If weaker, avoid them

If double their
strength, divide them

If 5 times stronger,
attack them

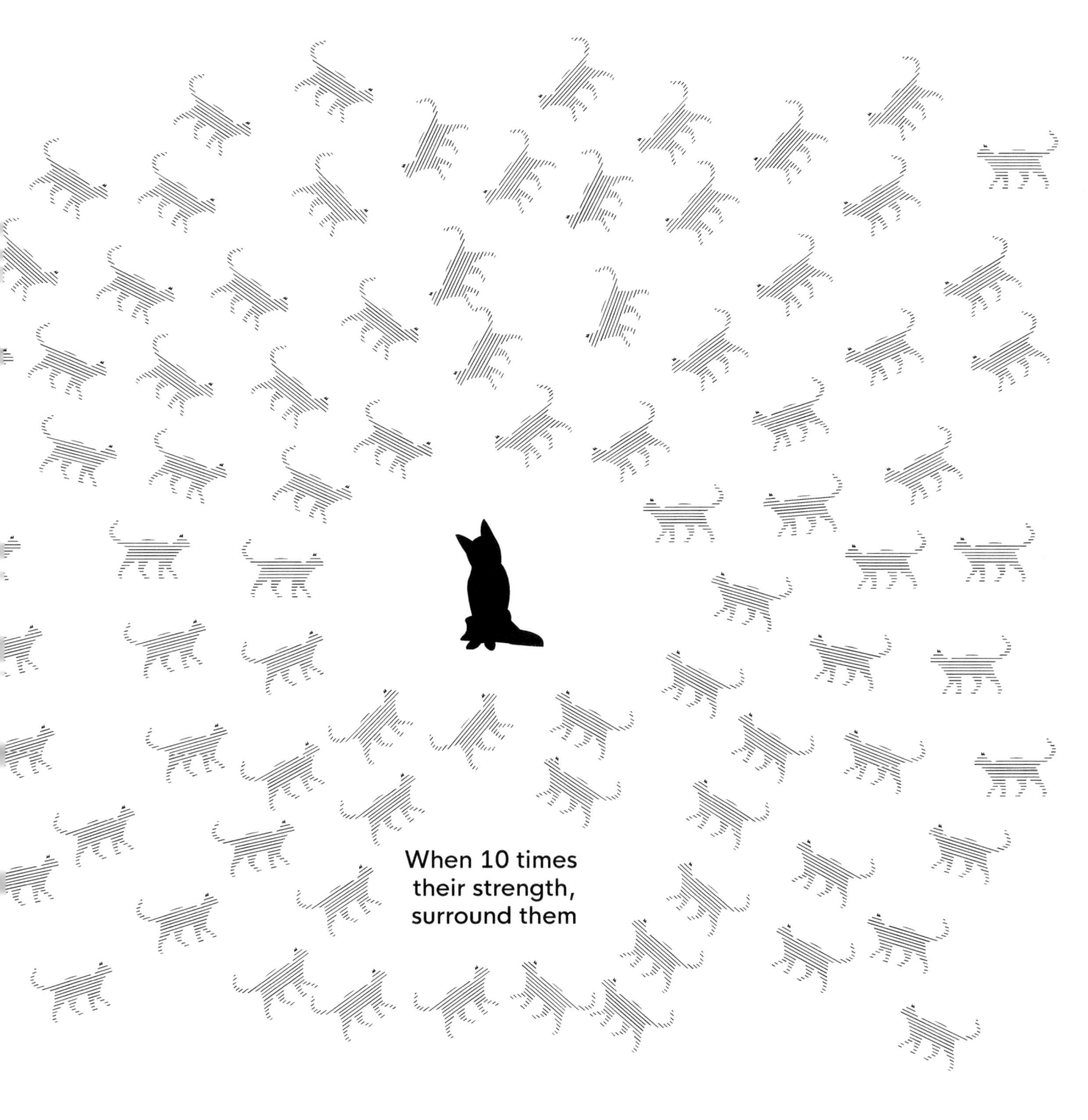

When 10 times
their strength,
surround them

#4 Understand Deception

The basic quality of any strategic operation.

Pretend to be
incompetent

Make yourself
seem close when
still far away

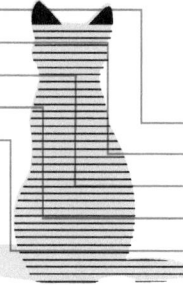

Hit when it's
unexpected

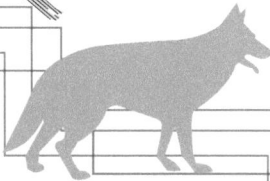

Set one party
against another
when united

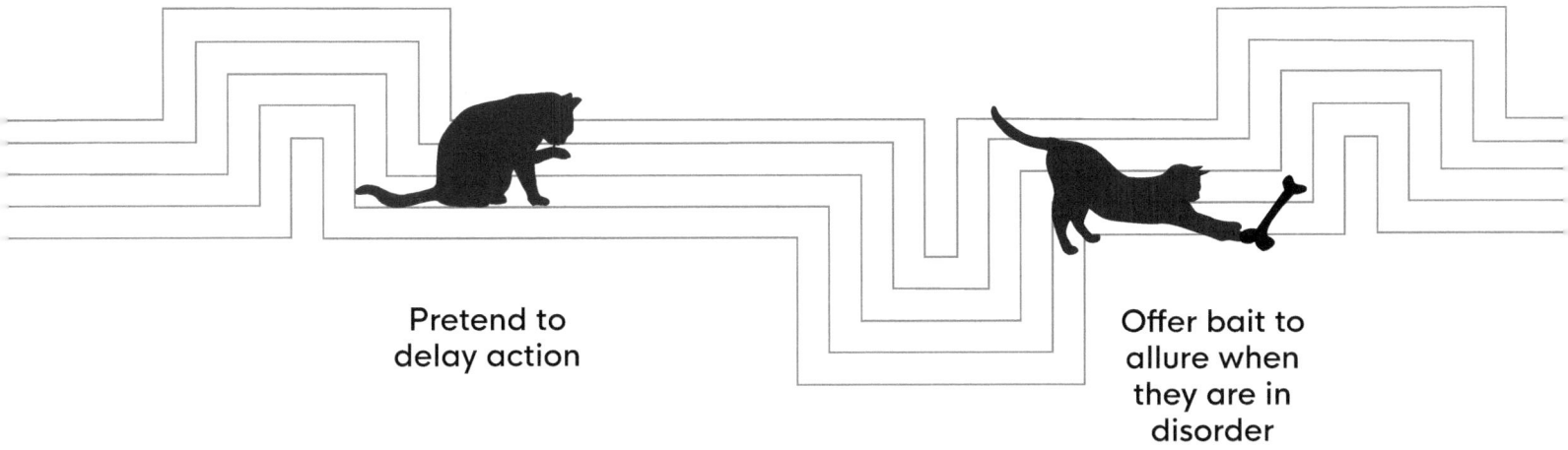

Pretend to
delay action

Offer bait to
allure when
they are in
disorder

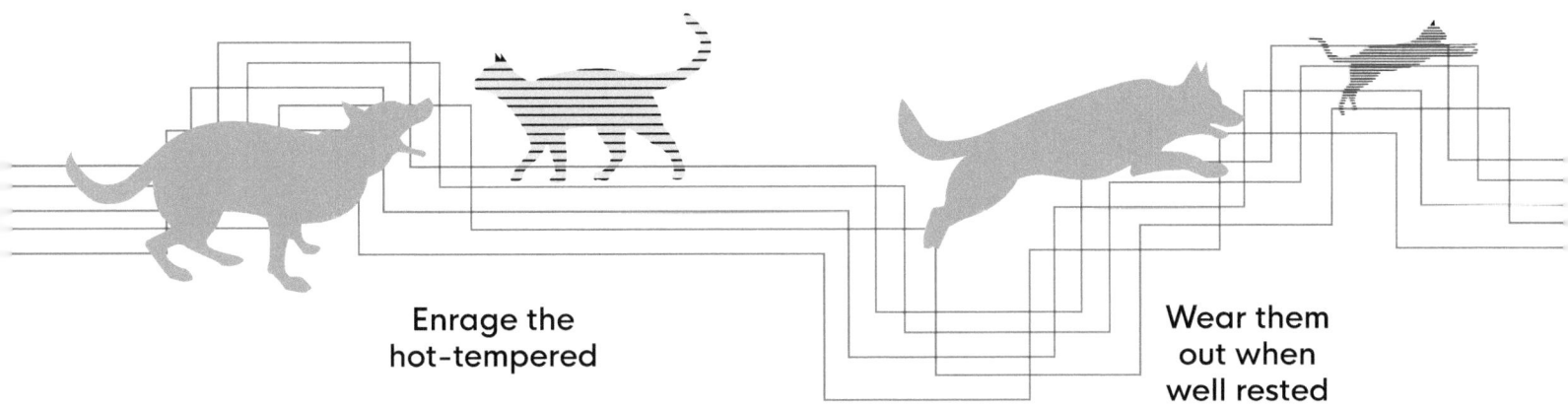

Enrage the
hot-tempered

Wear them
out when
well rested

#5 Compare The 5 Factors

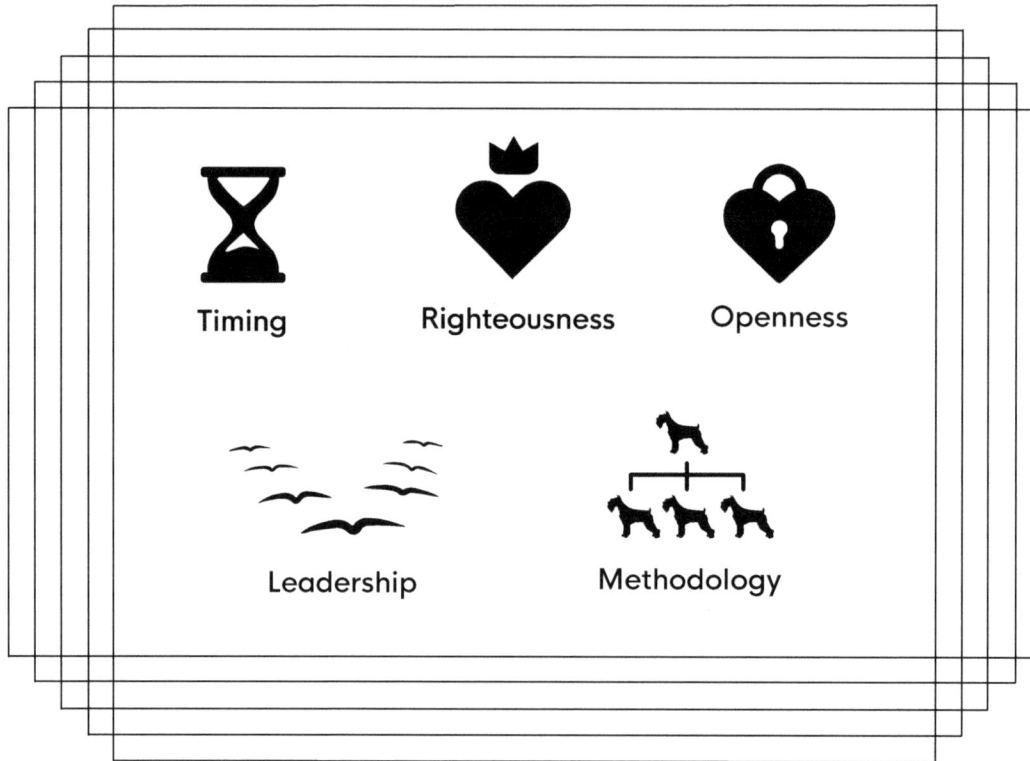

Timing

Righteousness

Openness

Leadership

Methodology

When confict occurs, compare the conditions
of ourselves and our opponent from the 5 factors
to forecast victory before the start of war.

Who will win this round?

#6 Make Calculations

10% eating

30% playing

60% sleeping

**Energy used
in Peaceful Times**

10% fighting

10% playing

10% eating

10% licking wounds

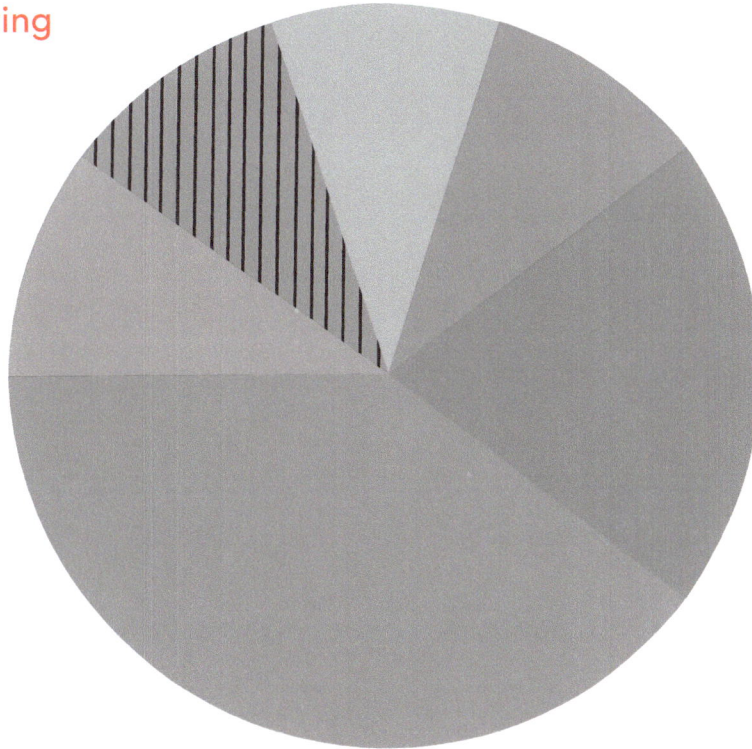

20% sleeping

40% strategizing

Energy used in War Time

#7 Different Paths to the Heart

Figure out which path your opponent has placed you on.

Distant Path
It is not easy to provoke a battle on this path. It is disadvantageous to fight

Hindering Path
Disadvantageous to both parties. It is an atmosphere of defeat. Even if the enemy gives bait, don't take it, pretend to retrat, strike when half-way in pursuit

Friendly Path
There are no unnecessary barriers here. Here you can grow freely. Remember to analyze people's motives carefully

Entrapping Path
Easy to enter, difficult to get out from. You can only strike when the enemy is not prepared

Steep Path
Take a high position
and wait for the enemy
to come. If they have
control over this path,
don't fight over it

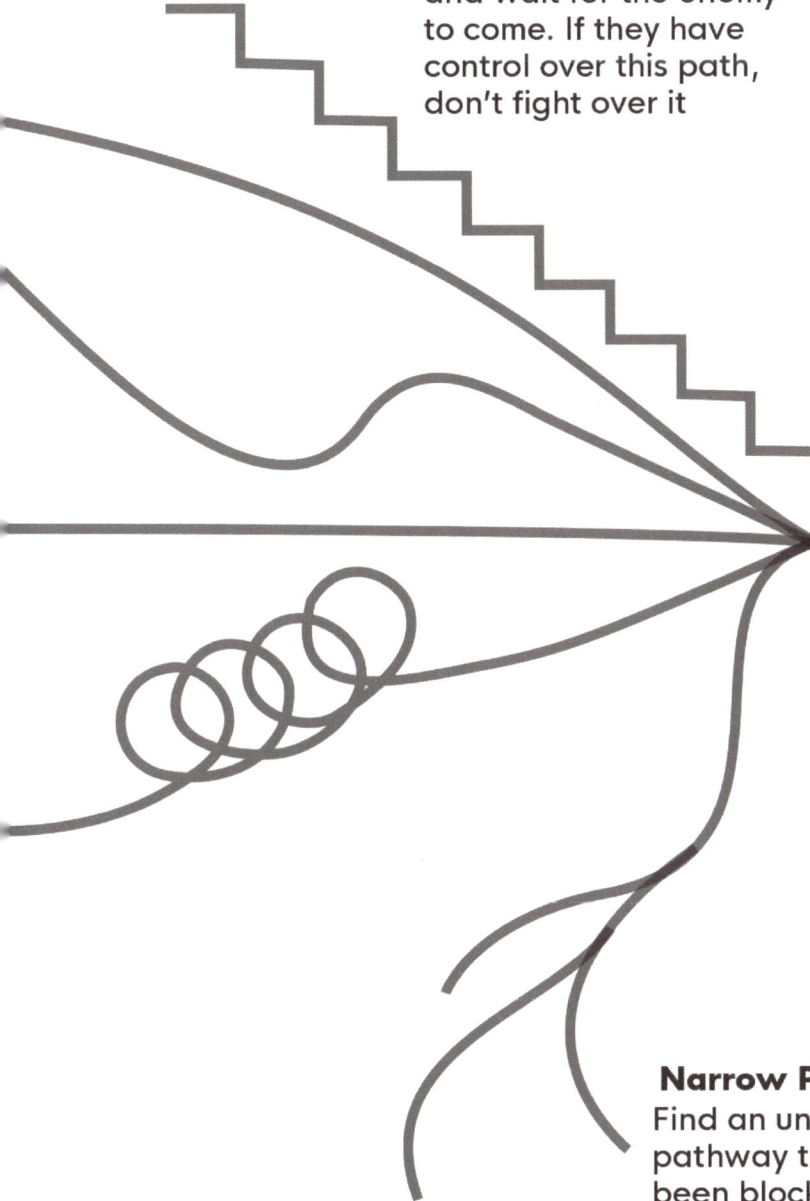

Narrow Path
Find an unoccupied
pathway that hos not
been blocked by the
enemy. From there,
find a way to advance

#8 Master the Tactic of Deviation

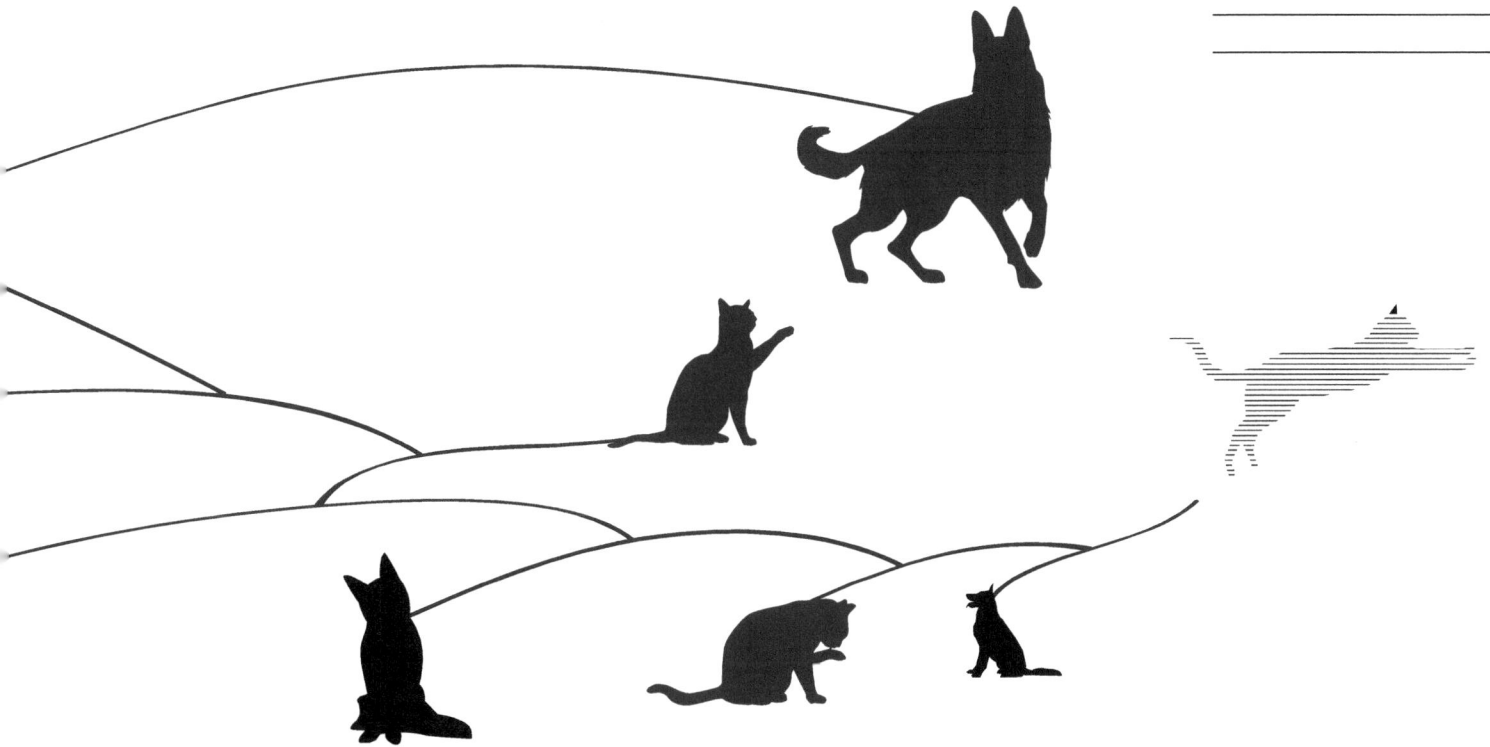

Weigh the pros and cons before you move.
Allocate your energy to suit your needs.
Diverge from the crowd.

#9 Build Momentum

Keep making progress. Every win counts.

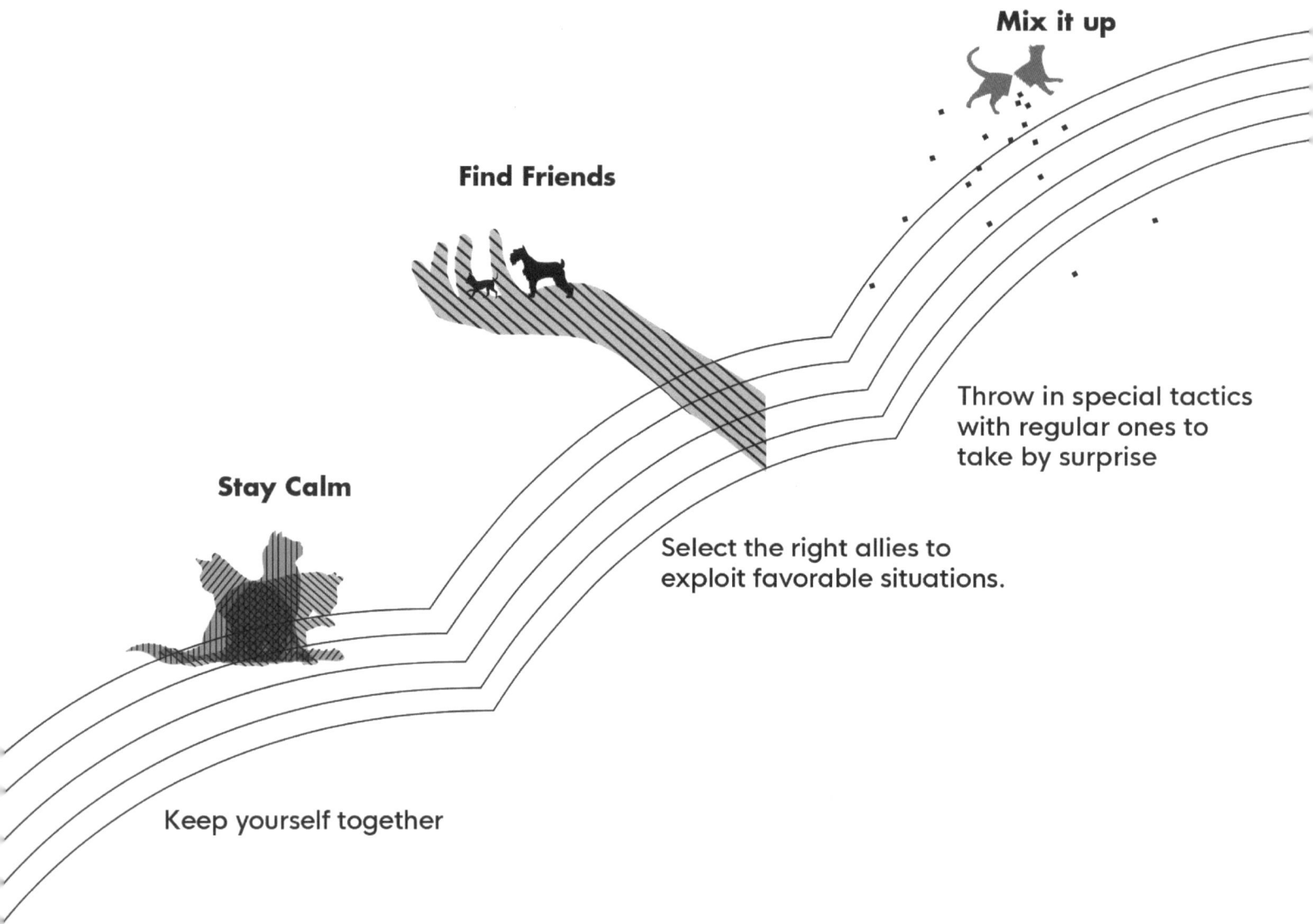

Mix it up

Find Friends

Stay Calm

Throw in special tactics
with regular ones to
take by surprise

Select the right allies to
exploit favorable situations.

Keep yourself together

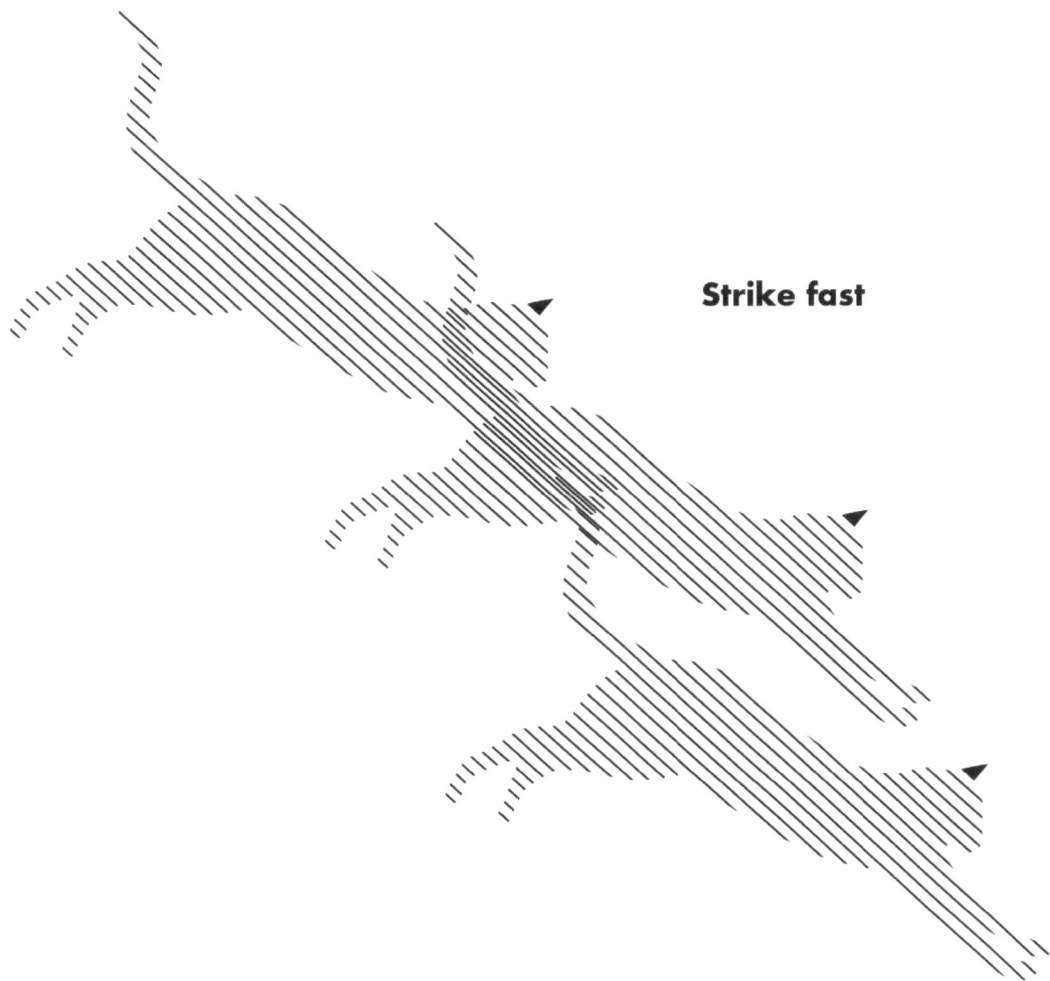

Strike fast

Choose an advantageous position and launch a swift and sharp attack.

#10 Interpret Behavior

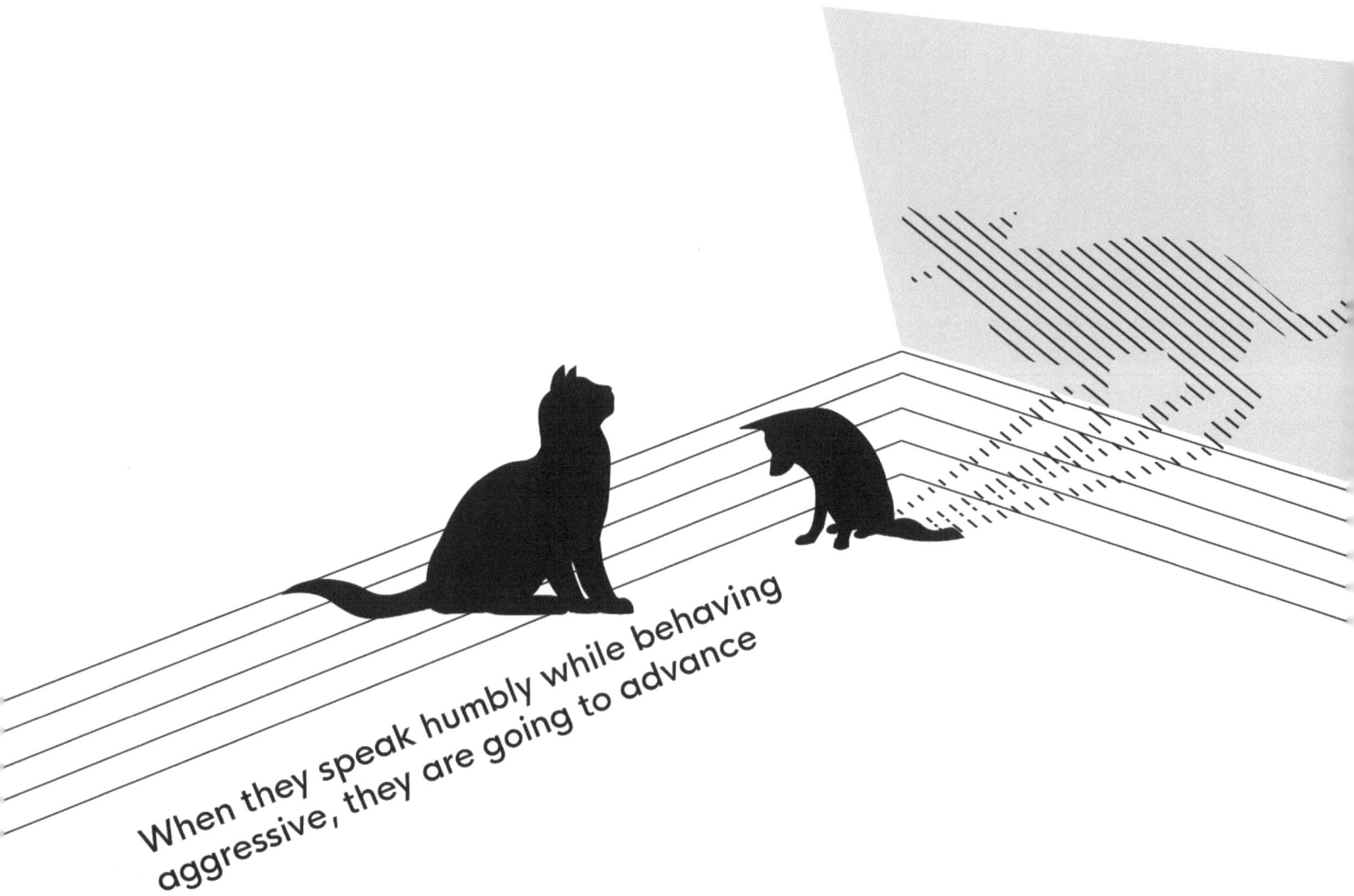

When they speak humbly while behaving aggressive, they are going to advance

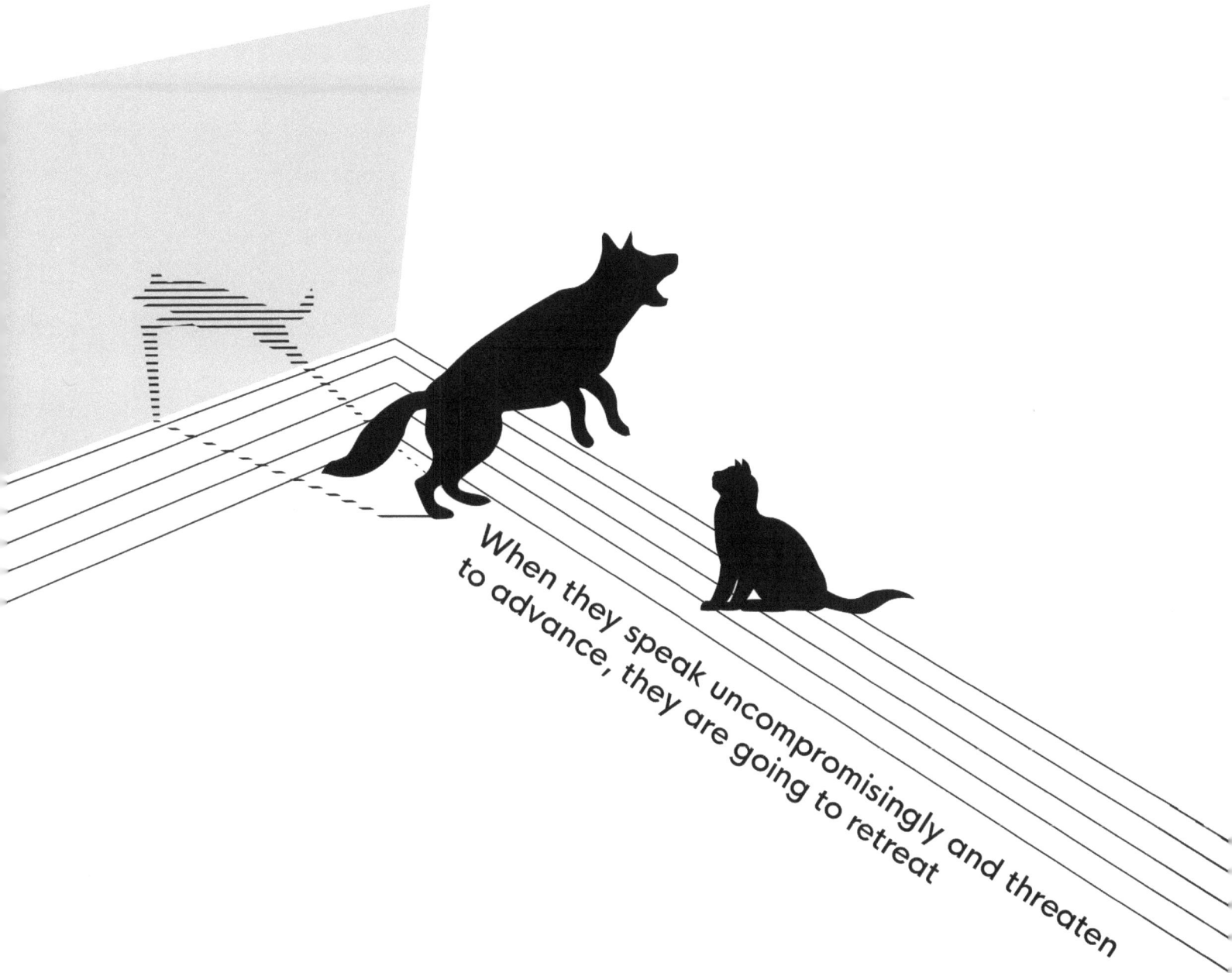

When they speak uncompromisingly and threaten to advance, they are going to retreat

#11 Gaining Advantage

Plan for a Victorious Disposition

Reel in the Results

Win first, then go to war,
not the other way around

Defeating your enemy
depends on their errors

Lead the Enemy by the Nose

When you are one step ahead of the game, you will be at ease; the later comer moving in haste will be weary

#12 Finding Balance

Weigh the Situations

When in a favorable position take full account of unfavorable factors to succeed in your plans.

When in an unfavorable position, take full account of favorable conditions to resolve difficulties

Coordination

If you cannot grasp a situation correctly, your left paw cannot help your right, let alone look for help

Limitations

When you take precautions in front, your rear will be weak.

If you strengthen everywhere, you will be weak everywhere

The Defensive and Offensive

When there is no chance of winning, take a defensive position.

When there is a chance, launch an attack

#13 Know the 9 War Grounds

Serious ground

Getting here required a "fight to the death attitude." These are the enemy's deep inner grounds. Plunder for provisions

Desperate ground

Make a speedy and desperate battle here or be destroyed

Open ground

Land accessible to both the enemy and yourself. Don't let communication get blocked. Defend yourself carefully

Encircled ground

Access is constricted, return requires detour. Ambush the

Dispersive ground

Your territory. Unify your will, do not fight here

Focal ground

First to gain control acquires the support of other peers. Form alliances

Frontier ground

Initial entry into enemy grounds. Keep going, be alert and maintain top performance

Difficult ground

Hard place to make moves, pass through swiftly.

Contentious ground

Never attack those who reached here first

strong. Devise escape plans, block the points of access.

#14 The 5 Fatal Weaknesses

You will be defeated if you are the brave, unresourceful and desperate fighter. You will be captured if you cling to things that don't serve you. You will make regretful moves if you are quick-tempered. You will be shamed and driven to reckless action if you are too proud. You will be hesitant and passive if you are too benevolent.

#15 Beware of the 5 Advances

There are some groups that should not be captured

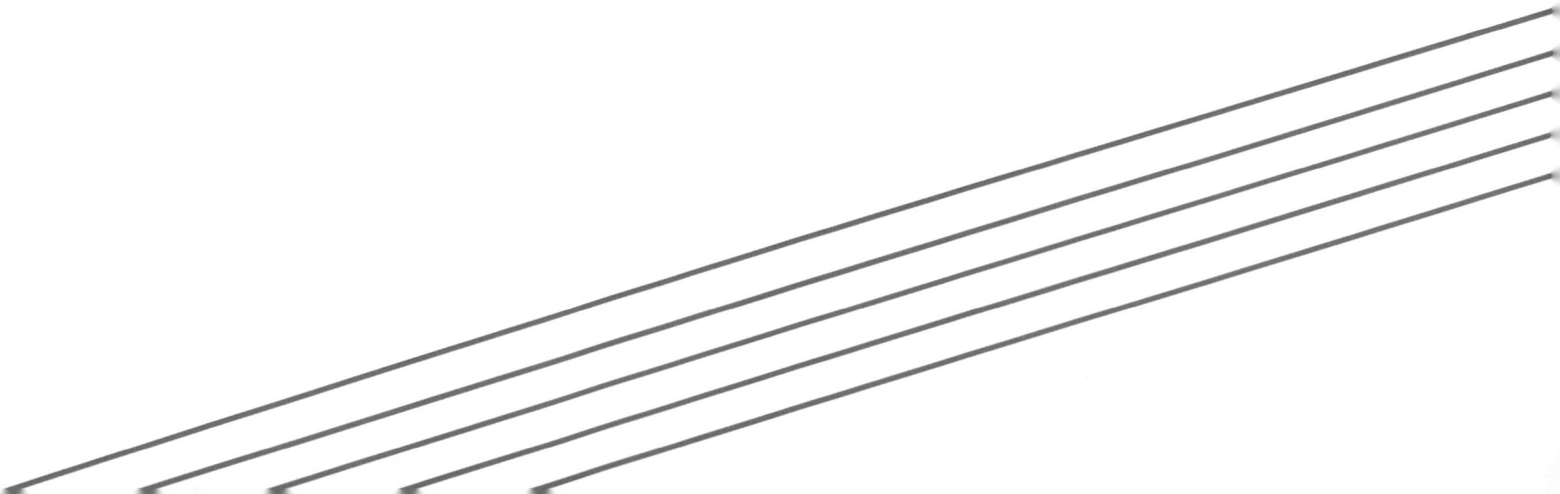

There are some that should not be attacked

There are some fights that
should not be won

There are some orders that
need not be obeyed

There are some
roads that should
not be followed

Conclusion

Knowing the strategies of war has made Misty confident and ready to face her fears...

Does this mean he wants to be friends?!

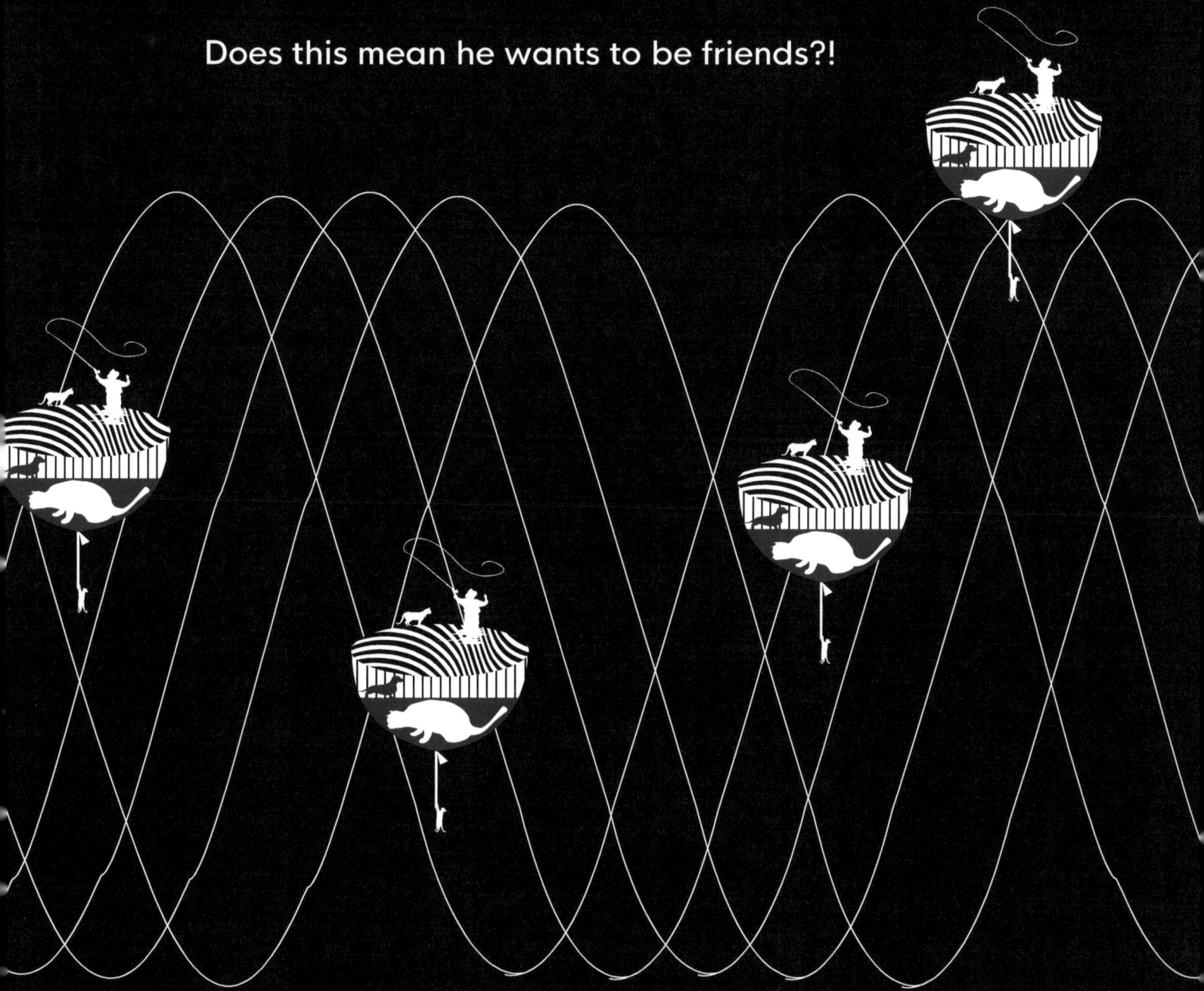

www.ingramcontent.com/pod-product-compliance
Lightning Source LLC
LaVergne TN
LVHW072052070426
835508LV00002B/66